Matthew Vickery

Implications of Edward Said's Orientalism (1978) for the social scientific study of the contemporary Middle East

Der GRIN Verlag publiziert seit 1998 wissenschaftliche Arbeiten von Studenten, Hochschullehrern und anderen Akademikern als eBook und gedrucktes Buch. Die Verlagswebsite www.grin.com ist die ideale Plattform zur Veröffentlichung von Hausarbeiten, Abschlussarbeiten, wissenschaftlichen Aufsätzen, Dissertationen und Fachbüchern.

Document Nr. V208957

Matthew Vickery

Implications of Edward Said's Orientalism (1978) for the social scientific study of the contemporary Middle East

GRIN Verlag

Die Deutsche Bibliothek verzeichnet diese Publikation in der Deutschen Nationalbibliografie; detaillierte bibliografische Daten sind im Internet über http://dnb.d-nb.de/ abrufbar.

1. Auflage 2012
Copyright © 2012 GRIN Verlag GmbH
http://www.grin.com
Druck und Bindung: Books on Demand GmbH, Norderstedt Germany
ISBN 978-3-656-36628-7

The implications of Edward Said's *Orientalism* (1978) for the social scientific study of the

contemporary Middle East

Over thirty years since its publication, and ten since the death of its author Edward Said, *Orientalism* (1978) continues to have a profound effect on Middle East studies; discovering the true or *underlying* implications of which will be the remit of this essay. *Orientalism* positioned Said as one of the founders and chief authorities in postcolonial criticism, opening the 'floodgate[s] . . . that breached the authority of Western scholarship on Other societies' (Prakash, 1995: 99); consequently work produced in the field since has often been in response to Said's scholarship (Sullivan, Ismael,1991: 2). Through adopting Michel Foucault's concept of discourse and Antonio Gramsci's notion of hegemonic culture, Said's study charts the concept of 'Orientalism'* - the study of the Orient, especially the Islamic, and Arab world - as a 'corporate institution' (1978: 13) formed by the West, or 'Occident,' through encompassing 'a set of generalizations, structures, relationships [and] texts' (Schaar, 2000: 181) which created a discourse, in which the Occident deals with *and* defines the Orient. Crucially Said, embracing Foucault, emphasises the 'closeness' between this discourse and politics (Said, 1978: 96), arguing that Orientalism (knowledge) as a discourse was a vital factor in the Occident's imperial conquests (power) and ambitions in the Orient.** Vitally, Said's critique fundamentally pushed criticism of Orientalism out with the disciplinary boundaries of which it had been restricted previously (Sardar, 1999: 65-66). As such, the combination of the above has led *Orientalism* to become a canon in Middle East studies. Significantly however, an enduring question remains: with such a startling critique of Orientalism as an academic discipline, what does

---

* As an important note regarding terms and to avoid confusion: *Orientalism,* is to denote Said's 1978 book; Orientalism, denotes the academic discipline of studying the Orient from the position of an academic in the West (Occident); an Orientalist, is an individual who studies Orientalism; 'Orientalist' or 'Orientalism', are direct references to Said's negative connotations of Orientalism as an academic discipline. For example: He was an Orientalist, regards an individual studying the academic discipline of Orientalism; He was an 'Orientalist', regards an individual who holds the negative views of the Orient that Said defines in *Orientalism*. Furthermore the terms 'Occident' and 'West', will be used interchangeably in this essay; when discussing France and the UK, the term 'Europe' is also used. The term 'Middle East' is used separately at times from 'Orient', but the former can be regarded as part of the latter.
** Said, as he acknowledges, was not the first person to critique Orientalism as an academic field; however noteworthy is that he was not the first to discuss Orientalism as a discourse of power as well (see Hodgson, 1993; a collection of essays from 1940-60, albeit not through Foucauldian language).

Orientalism imply, and thus what are the implications of Orientalism, for the social scientific study of the contemporary Middle East. This question, at the 'core of the argument around 'Orientalism'' (Halliday, 1993: 145), is the impetus for this essay, and will be tackled through two undertakings. First, a full and concise explanation of Said's theory and argument in *Orientalism* will be explored, with particular emphasis on the all-encompassing discourse Said attributes to Orientalism, which creates the dichotomy of Orient and Occident, East and West, "us" and "them"; as well as how this Foucauldian notion of discourse is seen vis-à-vis Western colonialisation and imperialism in the Middle East. From this, it will be shown what *Orientalism* implies to the study of the Middle East if Said's theory is taken in its entirety as fact: the study of the Orient from the Occident will always be flawed. This essay's second section however, will look critically at Said's theory, using scholarly criticism to find faults and contradictions, in order to sort the wheat from the chaff. The consequences will be a discovery of what the real or *underlying* implications of *Orientalism* are for the social scientific study of the Middle East. Through this two pronged approach, *Orientalism* can be unpackaged, then placed back together again, filtering out the parts that do not stand up to scrutiny; thus allowing for the truest and most accurate discussion concerning what *Orientalism* implies regarding the study of the contemporary Middle East.

The Implications of Said's *Orientalism*

For Said, 'Orientalism is a style of thought based upon the ontological and epistemological distinction made between "the Orient" and (most of the time) "the Occident."' (*ibid*: 2). This style of thought, the acceptance of a distinction between Orient and Occident (with the Orient as the antithesis of the 'civilised', 'cultured' Occident, or West), encompasses a 'large mass of writers', including 'poets, novelists, philosophers, political theorists and imperial administrators.' (*ibid*: 3); thus creating a 'political vision of reality' promoting a very real difference 'between the familiar (Europe, the West, "us") and the strange (the Orient, the East, "them")' (*ibid*: 43). Said argues that this discourse has existed from the time of Homer to Marx, right through to the present day. Thus a 'corporate

institution' has been created by the West, which defines and deals with the Orient, 'by making statements about it, teaching it, settling it, ruling over it'; in brief, a Western discourse 'for dominating, restructuring, and having authority over the Orient' (*ibid*: 1-3). Therefore the Orient cannot be a subject that involves freedom of thought. Indeed Said states this explicitly when describing the modern 'Orientalist':

> 'As a judge of the Orient, the modern Orientalist does not, as he believes and even says, stand apart from it objectively. His human detachment, whose sign is the absence of sympathy covered by professional knowledge, is weighted heavily with all the orthodox attitudes, perspectives, and moods of Orientalism that I have been describing.' (*ibid:* 104)

Therefore an individual (from the West) cannot separate themselves from the orthodox perspective of the Orient; it is inscribed in their very being, and even those whose profession is to treat their subject with objectivity cannot do so. At the very core of the relationship between Orient and Occident is thus this dichotomy, a binary opposition holding the Occident in high regard, and the Orient as merely existing, and always in the formers shadow. The omnipotence of this discourse and dichotomy was such, that no writer could escape from it (Zarnett, 2008: 51). The implications of Said's argument is thus: an individual from the Occident *cannot* truly write objectively about any aspect of the Orient, as their writings, even if written to be objective, will always be tainted with a negative (mis) representation of the Orient that has, and continues to be, dominant in Western discourse[*]. Therefore in brief, if Said's argument is taken as truth and in its entirety, *Orientalism* implies that social scientific study based in the West, cannot provide accurate, objective study of the Middle East; and in regards to the study of the contemporary Middle East, a social scientist, is not only part of the prevailing dominant discourse, but any sources or literature they may use, will also be tainted by this discourse (Said, 1978: 176-177).

---

[*] Said, near the end of *Orientalism,* claims that he does 'not believe in the limited proposition that only a black can write about blacks, a Muslim about Muslims and so forth' (Ibid: 322); yet this sentence contradicts Said's argument throughout which puts across the notion that the Orient and thus the subaltern is misrepresented by the Occident, and that the former can only ever misrepresent the latter.

Furthermore the mention of imperialism ('imperial') in the earlier quote is an important one. With Said's identification of a body of writing accredited as 'Orientalist', he also related this to the Foucauldian notion of discourse. Said argues that this 'internally structured archive built up from the literature [about the Orient]' (*ibid* : 58), 'can be put to political use' (*ibid* : 96); manifesting most obviously in the 19th and 20th century colonial enterprises of France and Britain in the Middle East, and most recently, America's post-World War Two imperial ambitions. Thus through Orientalism, as discussed previously, the Orient has been fashioned as a negative reversal of the West and its culture; the link to power is that this literature formed the West's knowledge of the Orient, and according to Said, this allowed the West to gain control over the East: knowledge equals power. Said shows this hypothesis in action:

> 'England knows Egypt, Egypt is what England knows; England knows that Egypt cannot have self-government; England confirms that by occupying Egypt; for the Egyptians, Egypt is what England has occupied and now governs; foreign occupation therefore becomes "the very basis" of contemporary Egyptian civilization; Egypt requires, indeed insists upon, British occupation.' (*ibid*: 34)

Here Said is illustrating the effect the body of 'Orientalist' scholarship holds: through literature, England has knowledge of Egypt and the literature places England above Egypt; the negative views of Egypt present in the literature promotes the idea of Egypt and the Orient as being unable to self-govern; this leads to occupation; which leads to the hierarchy in 'Orientalist' literature being realised in terms of physical power. As *Orientalism's* final section argues, this Foucauldian discourse of power continues to exist, albeit chiefly in the form of American imperialism, à la neo-conservative policies towards the Middle East. Thus for Said, governments who seek policy advice on the Middle East encounter the prevailing 'Orientalist' discourse, to such an extent, that 'if the Arab occupies space enough for attention, it is as a negative value' (*ibid:* 286); this occurs as modern 'Orientalists', Said's term for contemporary social scientists that study the Middle East, have taken 'over the attitudes of cultural hostility and kept them' (*ibid:* 290). Therefore, further to the inability of the social scientist to research and study the Middle East objectively, *Orientalism* also implies that the social

scientist through continuing the discourse of power and the misrepresentations about the Orient, feeds into the power structure of Western dominance over the Orient; most explicitly when advising government, most subtlety when simply carrying out their day-to-day profession. Therefore if *Orientalism* is taken as a whole, the argument within it implies that the chances of accurate, unbiased and worthwhile social scientific study of the contemporary Middle East is virtually non-existent. Thus for Said the social scientist studies through a distorted lens, purveying a reality of the Orient that only exists as a misrepresentation (Lockman, 2004: 185); while, acting (consciously or unconsciously) as an instrument of imperialism, and agent of the Western implemented hierarchy of power. This in black-and-white is what *Orientalism* implies, however as will be seen, the *underlying* implications of Said's argument are much less depressing for the social scientist, although still essential vis-à-vis the study of the Middle East. The social scientist may not need to pack his suitcase, but a rearrangement of his library is certainly recommended.

The *Underlying* Implications of Said's *Orientalism*

This essay so far has detailed what appears to be the fundamental inferences *Orientalism* implies for the social scientists study of the Middle East; however these specific implications can only manifest as true *if* the argument within the book is correct in full. What I am proposing is to find the *underlying* implications of *Orientalism*. To clarify, by using critiques of Said's argument, revealing the holes contained within it, a slim lined version of the argument will emerge, without the constituent parts that have been proved contradictory, incorrect or suspect. In this respect, the use of the term *underlying* denotes a set of implications that can be deduced rationally, constructed from a deconstruction of Said's argument, thus ensuring implications for the social scientist are not formed from misinformation or questionable fragments of the argument contained within *Orientalism*. From this, the true, real or *underlying* implications of Said's *Orientalism* will be exposed, providing a more valuable, focussed picture of what *Orientalism* implies to the study of the Middle East.

Considering the set-up of the first section of this essay, in logical fashion, Said's 'Orientalist' discourse will be considered first, exploring whether it stands up to factual scrutiny. It is no secret that Said has been often criticised for his (mis) use and non-use of sources within *Orientalism* to consolidate an argument that proclaims to have exposed a negative discourse towards the Orient since the age of Classical Greece (Clifford, 1980; Kopf, 1980; Macfie, 2002; Irwin, 2006). To show how *Orientalism* must be treated with care as well as intrigue, it is worth looking at the very beginning of *Orientalism*, in fact to the first quotation Said uses:

'They cannot represent themselves; they must be represented.' (Said, citing Karl Marx, 1978: xxvii)

Used at times throughout, Said seemingly implies that Marx is justifying the use of the 'Orientalist' discourse, because the Orient and its people cannot represent themselves, therefore the Occident must provide representation. The quotation's use in this context has received much criticism (Ahmad, 1992; Richardson, 1990, 2000; Macfie 2002; Habib, 2005). In its original context, the quote has no reference to the Orient, or European/Western representation of the Orient. Indeed it regards a disjointed group of 19th century peasants in France who were, due to a dire state of poverty, 'incapable of enforcing their class interests in their own name, whether through a parliament or through a convention. They cannot represent themselves, they must be represented' (Marx and Engels, 1973). This remark was 'not, as Said seemed to assume, a condition of imposed silence' (Richardson, 1990: 122). I am using this misuse of Marx explicitly to show that even from page one, *Orientalism* includes potential misuses of sources which must be taken into consideration when taking Said's argument as a whole.

Furthermore, in order to consolidate his argument regarding an all-encompassing 'Orientalist' discourse, Said classifies all who write about the Orient as doing so negatively (Plump, 1979). This however is a rather generalised and unfair statement[*]. To use Marx again as illustration, his literature

---

[*] To make such a declaration fairly, Said would have to have read all books produced on the Orient, (arguably) at least from the period 1800-1978. This in itself comprises more than 60,000 texts (Sivan, 1985), an impossible number to read. Said does state regarding the literature critiqued in *Orientalism*, that there was 'a much larger number that I simply had to leave out' (1978: 4). With this in mind, Said by claiming all writers on the Orient as

about India (the region of the Orient on which he published two books), says nothing different in terms of what he already says about Europe, and for the latter often in more venomous terms; indeed if Marx was powered by any discourse, it was not 'Orientalism', but the discourse of nineteenth century political economy (Ahmad, 1992:230). Hourani also rightly explains that Said, in his attempt to paint a discourse that has tainted all Europeans/Westerners writings on the Orient, has ignored the humanistic accomplishments of Orientalists such as Marshall Hodgson, Andre Raymond and Claude Cahen[**] (1979). Interestingly the only individual Said seems to regard in *Orientalism* as having uncorrupted scholarship is anthropologist Clifford Geertz (Said, 1978: 326); however seven years later, Said claims Geertz's work is 'standard disciplinary rationalizations and self-congratulatory clichés' (Said, 1985: 93). Said in the first instance provides no reason for praising Geertz, and second time round delivers no rational for his reverse decision, thus summing up the problem of Said's all-encompassing discourse: although many individuals Said highlights certainly portray negative and even racist views about the Orient (Rudyard Kipling, Sir William Jones, Lord Balfour; Bernard Lewis and Raphael Patai as more recent examples), those that do not easily fit into the same category or seem innocent to the observer, are often given little explanation as to why they are being regarded as an integral part of the 'Orientalist' discourse. Indeed, Said in *Culture and Imperialism* (1993), the follow-up to *Orientalism*, extends the 'Orientalist' label to such literally giants as Dickens, Austin and others. In this way, Said has effectively essentialised the Occident; ironically in the same manner he accuses the West of performing towards the Orient. Thus the method in which Said has construed 'the origins of Orientalism simply lends strength to the essentialistic categories of 'Orient' and 'Occident,' representing the ineradicable distinction between East and West, which [*Orientalism*] is ostensibly set on demolishing' (al-'Azm, 2000: 219). In summary, *Orientalism* may indeed imply that the social scientist cannot study the Middle East in an objective manner; however, although the basic premise of *Orientalism* unquestionably has merit (Kopf, 1980; Halliday, 1993), it is also guilty at times of

---

'Orientalist', even if he discovered a vast majority of the literature he read to be 'Orientalist' in nature can be seen as a basic generalisation; instead, Said should have noted the limitations in his study more obviously and accepted that he was generalising to an extent rather than providing objective truth.

[**] In the 1995 afterword to *Orientalism*, Said, in regards to Hourani (1979), claims this does not contradict his argument in *Orientalism* (2003 [1978]: 342). However by focusing just on the negatives, while not acknowledging that positives exist, is ignoring aspects that potentially contradict and undermine his argument.

misusing and misinterpreting sources and writers, misstating facts[*], and crucially of essentialising the Occident to such an extent that Said, for the sake of his argument, cannot claim any writers as being unaffected by the discourse he outlines. The *underlying* implications of *Orientalism* vis-à-vis this discourse are thus: the study of the contemporary Middle East is possible when approached with care, indeed a promising benefit of Said's book is that a new generation of social scientists look on previous sources and literature with more scrutiny (Adams, 1997). *Orientalism* therefore implies the need for a wakeup call to the potential bias nature of text for social scientists, and Said does an admirable job in highlighting the wide-ranging extent of this. Though he also attempts to create a category encompassing all who write on the Orient as doing so with a shared negative discourse, whether subconscious or not; this is a rather simple generalisation. This critical analysis shows that Said has gone too far in essentialising the Occident, through the creation of an essentialised 'European Mind', yet the *underlying* implications still show value for the social scientist in Said's *Orientalism* concerning the social scientific study of the contemporary Middle East.

Having discovered the problems with the 'Orientalist' discourse Said proposes, questions can now be asked regarding whether knowledge equals power in the way Said sets out in *Orientalism*. To do so, it has substance to reflect on Said's basic argument that any notion of the Orient coming from the Occident must be a misrepresentation formed from an all-encompassing 'Orientalist' discourse (which has now been critiqued). However there is a fundamental flaw regarding this argument and Said's connection of it to Foucault's notion of a discourse of power. Indeed, if all representations of the Orient were misrepresentations, this must surely produce false knowledge; yet it seems unfathomable to think that the successful (and undeniably at times brutal) colonisation of the Middle East by the United Kingdom and France could have been so effective if all knowledge gained was false. Therefore if, as Said claims, Orientalism is just a set of representations, not reflecting the 'true

---

[*] Two examples include: Said's claim that the UK and France 'dominated' the Levant in the latter 17th century (18), when it was still very much under the control of the Ottoman empire; Said calling Egypt a British "colony" (36), where in reality it was always a protectorate, the differences between the two being substantial enough that they should not be used as synonymous.

Orient'[*] yet it was a "corporate institution" used in imperial conquest and governance, there must have therefore, at the very least, been a time when there existed an overlap between the Orient as a representation and the 'real' Orient; if not, Said's claim that Orientalism was used as a discourse of power must be false (Young, 1990: 129). Furthermore concerning knowledge and power, Said fails to note other rational or strategic explanations for French and British military manoeuvres in the Middle East; as one example, Said remarks that the 'Suez Canal idea' was 'the logical conclusion of Orientalist thought and effort', (Said, 1978: 91) rather than the more probable explanation regarding the Anglo-French imperial rivalry at the time. That is not to say that an 'Orientalist' discourse could have been used as partial justification for military maneuverers; however this cannot be regarded as full-on justification or rational. Lastly, Said also conveniently ignores German Orientalism throughout the book, the literature of which comprised a significant body of Orientalist scholarship. The reason for Said's omission is straightforward: Germany had no real imperial presence in the Orient; as such knowledge clearly did not produce power in a Foucauldian sense. Germany is thus a counterexample to Said's theory, showing that 'the lines of scholarly inquiry and political power. . . [do] not always meet' (Prakash, 1995: 202). Therefore, if knowledge does not always equal power as Said claims in *Orientalism* and as shown above, then it is possible for the social scientific study of the contemporary Middle East to exist without the social scientist intentionally or unintentionally consolidating Western hegemony over the Orient. However, despite setting out to find the flaws in *Orientalism*, that does not mean Said is completely incorrect in his conclusions; contemporary examples do exist of Said's 'Orientalist' discourse being wielded in order to justify power over the Middle East, two obvious examples include the power of the Israel Lobby in the United States[**] and American foreign policy towards the Middle East after 9/11.[***] However to conclude that Said was correct in *Orientalism* to

---

[*] Said makes references to a "true" or "real" Orient on pages 21-22, 67 and 203 of *Orientalism*. The book is rather confused as to whether a "real" Orient does exist, however on page 322, Said tries to cover his back by stating: 'It is not the thesis of this book to suggest that there is such a thing as a real of true Orient (Islam, Arab, or whatever).'
[**] AIPAC (The American Israel Public Affairs Committee) as one example, the most powerful lobby group dedicated to Israel in the US political system, has been very successful in portraying Palestinians through Said's 'Orientalist' discourse in order to achieve Israeli interests. See: 'The Israel Lobby' (Mearsheimer and Walt, 2008)
[***] By itself this may be debatable, as US foreign policy has for many years been influenced to a certain extent by neo-conservatism. However in the aftermath of the 9/11 attacks, the discourse of a Judeo-Christian West

state that any knowledge (even false knowledge, which is what Said implies despite the contradiction) gained of the Orient would transform into power against the Orient could be regarded as naïve. When Said's argument is looked at through a critical lens, different implications (the *'underlying'* implications) do occur from a non-critical stance on *Orientalism*. That is, this critiqued version of *Orientalism* still implies the continued use of a discourse of power particularly in the United States, as does the non-critiqued version of *Orientalism* looked at in the first section. Yet, it is not all prevailing, and the modern social scientist *can* produce objective knowledge of the Middle East (and reject the 'Orientalist' discourse), however conversely they still also have the potential to produce dubious or bias knowledge and possibly, whether intended or not, be a factor in negative policy towards the Middle East through misrepresenting the region.

Conclusion: Moving Forward

For students and scholars who study the contemporary Middle East, Said's *Orientalism* continues to be regarded as a keystone text. As a theoretical framework, *Orientalism* can provide valuable tools to the social scientist for contemporary Middle East study, and in this respect Edward Said should be commended. Discovering these tools, i.e. what *Orientalism* implies, has been the remit of this essay. If one takes the argument of *Orientalism* in its entirety, the book implies that the social scientist should be made redundant, being unable to separate misrepresentations of the Orient from fact, while conversely helping to secure Western power over the Orient. However by critiquing Said's argument, it has been possible to illustrate that these initial implications cannot manifest as true due to two major flaws in *Orientalism*: Said's 'Orientalist' discourse cannot be regarded as all encompassing, and knowledge does not always equal power in the way Said sets out. However this does not mean that *Orientalism* has no merit. By critiquing Said's argument through siphoning the generalisations, misuses of sources, and at times the confused and repetitive polemic, it has been possible to discover the *underlying* implications of *Orientalism*. The discourse outlined in *Orientalism*

---

verses a (backwards and violent) Islamic East become more prevalent and much more noticeable in America's foreign policy towards the Middle East.

has existed, and still does exist, yet a social scientist does not need to be bound by it, and *can* produce objective knowledge about the Orient; to do so however requires rigorous scholarly consideration, and attention must be paid regarding research, literature, sources and writers used. Furthermore, in cases where the 'Orientalist' discourse does exist, it can be used as a form of power. Despite this the social scientist *can* distance himself from this by avoiding Said's 'Orientalist' discourse; however when government and scholarship overlap, the potential of knowledge equalling power in the Foucauldian sense seems far more likely. In brief, this essay has shown that what *Orientalism* really implies to the social scientific study is the realisation that 'human life does not conform to abstract theory' (Ashcroft, Ahluwalia, 1999: 7); there is no such thing as an 'Arab' mind, or indeed a 'European' one. This is despite Said's unfortunate generalisation of the Occident at times, while trying to explain the generalisation of the Orient; a further reason for delving through *Orientalism* in order to discover the *underlying* implications rather than taking the whole of Said's argument as correct. *Orientalism* has shown that Western study of the Middle East can still result at times in a dichotomous discourse of "us" and "them," as such, dangers regarding objective study still exist and should be tackled. As a world completely extinct of the 'Orientalist' discourse may not be possible in the near future, the only way to move forward from the current impasse involves social scientists taking on board the *underlying* implications of *Orientalism*; by doing so a new discourse will begin to evolve. Cantwell Smith provides the outline for this process, a plan that has always existed, but just needs to be implemented: following the dialogue of "us" and "them", 'the next step is dialogue, where "we" talk to "you". If there is listening and mutuality, this may become "we" talk *with* "you". The culmination of this progress is when "we all" are talking *with* each other about "us"' (1976: 142). Only when the *underlying* implications of *Orientalism* have been registered and acted upon by social scientists studying the Middle East can the dialogue make a complete shift from "us" and "them", to "us".

Word Count: 3817

Bibliography

Adams, P. 1997. 'Interview with Edward Said'. *Australian Broadcasting Corporation.*

Ahmad, A. 1992. *In Theory, Classes, Nations, Literatures.* (London: Verso)

Al-'Azm, S. J. 2000. 'Orientalism and Orientalism in Reverse.' in Macfie, A. L. *Orientalism: A Reader.* (Cambridge: Edinburgh University Press)

Ashcroft, P. Ahluwalia. 1999. *Edward Said: The Paradox of Identity.* (London: Routledge)

Cantwell Smith, W. 1976. 'Comparative Religion: Whither and Why?' in Oxtoby, W. G. *Religious Diversity: Essays by Wilfred Cantwell Smith.* (New York: Harper & Row)

Clifford, J. 1980. 'Review of *Orientalism*'. *History and Theory.* Vol. 19 (2): 204-223

Habib, I. 2005. 'Critical notes on Edward Said'. *Indian Journal Social Scientist,* vol 33, no 1

Halliday, F. 1993. 'Orientalism and Its Critics', *British Journal of Middle Eastern Studies.* Vol. 20 (2): 145-163

Hodgson, M. G. *Rethinking World History.* (Cambridge: Cambridge University Press)

Hourani, A. 1979. 'The Road to Morrocco', *New York Review of Books.* 27-30

Irwin, R. 2006. *For Lust of Knowing.* (London: Allen Lane)

Kopf, D. 1980. 'Hermeneutics versus History', *Journal of Asian Studies.* Vol. 39 (3): 495-506

Lockman, Z. 2004. *Contending Visions of the Middle East: The History and Politics of Orientalism.* (Cambridge: Cambridge University Press)

Macfie, A. L. 2002. *Orientalism.* (London: Pearson Education)

Mark, K. Engels, F. 1973. *Selected Works Vol. I.* (London: Progress)

Mearsheimer, J. J. Walt, S. M. 2008. *The Israel Lobby and US Foreign Policy.* (London: Penguin)

Plump, J. H. 1979. 'Review of *Orientalism*'. *New York Times Book Review.*

Prakash, G. 1995. 'Orientalism Now'. *History and Theory.* Vol. 34 (3): 199-212

Richardson, M. 1990. 'Enough Said – Reflections on Orientalism', *Anthropology Today*. Vol. 6 (4): 16-19

Richardson, M. 2000. 'Enough Said' in Macfie, A. L. *Orientalism: A Reader.* (Cambridge: Edinburgh University Press)

Said, E. 1978 [2003]. *Orientalism.* (London: Penguin)

Said, E. 1985. 'Orientalism Revisited' in Barker, F. *Europe and its Other.* (Colchester: University of Essex): 89-107

Said, E (1993). *Culture and Imperialism.* (London: Vintage)

Sardar, Z. 1999. *Orientalism.* (Buckingham: Open University Press)

Schaar, S. 2000. 'Orientalism at the Service of Imperialism' in Macfie, A. L. *Orientalism: A Reader.* (Cambridge: Edinburgh University Press)

Sivan, E. 1985. *Interpretations of Islam: Past and Present.* (Princeton: Darwin Press)

Sullivan, E. L. Ismael, J. S. 1991. *The Contemporary Study of the Arab World.* (Alberta: University of Alberta Press)

Young, R. 1990. *White Mythologies: Writing History and the West.* (London: Routledge)

Zarnett, D. 2008. 'Review of 'Defending the West: A Critique of Edward Said's *Orientalism*'' *Democratiya.* Vol.12 (1): 50-61